1.5

SUPER CUTE!

Baby
Camels

by Megan Borgert-Spaniol

BLASTOFF! READERS

BELLWETHER MEDIA • MINNEAPOLIS, MN

Note to Librarians, Teachers, and Parents:

Blastoff! Readers are carefully developed by literacy experts and combine standards-based content with developmentally appropriate text.

Level 1 provides the most support through repetition of high-frequency words, light text, predictable sentence patterns, and strong visual support.

Level 2 offers early readers a bit more challenge through varied simple sentences, increased text load, and less repetition of high-frequency words.

Level 3 advances early-fluent readers toward fluency through increased text and concept load, less reliance on visuals, longer sentences, and more literary language.

Level 4 builds reading stamina by providing more text per page, increased use of punctuation, greater variation in sentence patterns, and increasingly challenging vocabulary.

Level 5 encourages children to move from "learning to read" to "reading to learn" by providing even more text, varied writing styles, and less familiar topics.

Whichever book is right for your reader, Blastoff! Readers are the perfect books to build confidence and encourage a love of reading that will last a lifetime!

This edition first published in 2017 by Bellwether Media, Inc.

No part of this publication may be reproduced in whole or in part without written permission of the publisher. For information regarding permission, write to Bellwether Media, Inc., Attention: Permissions Department, 5357 Penn Avenue South, Minneapolis, MN 55419.

Library of Congress Cataloging-in-Publication Data

Names: Borgert-Spaniol, Megan, 1989- author.
Title: Baby Camels / by Megan Borgert-Spaniol.
Other titles: Blastoff! Readers. 1, Super Cute!
Description: Minneapolis, MN : Bellwether Media, Inc., [2017] | Series: Blastoff! Readers. Super Cute! | Audience: Ages 5-8. | Audience: K to grade 3. | Includes bibliographical references and index.
Identifiers: LCCN 2015043276 | ISBN 9781626173873 (hardcover : alk. paper)
Subjects: LCSH: Camels–Infancy–Juvenile literature.
Classification: LCC QL737.U54 B664 2017 | DDC 599.63/62–dc23
LC record available at http://lccn.loc.gov/2015043276

Printed in the United States of America, North Mankato, MN.

Table of Contents

Camel Calf!

A baby camel
is called a calf.
It is born with a
thick **wool** coat.

The **newborn** calf
lies next to mom.
Mom **nuzzles**
her baby.

Standing Up

The calf tries to
stand soon after
birth. It starts on
its back legs.

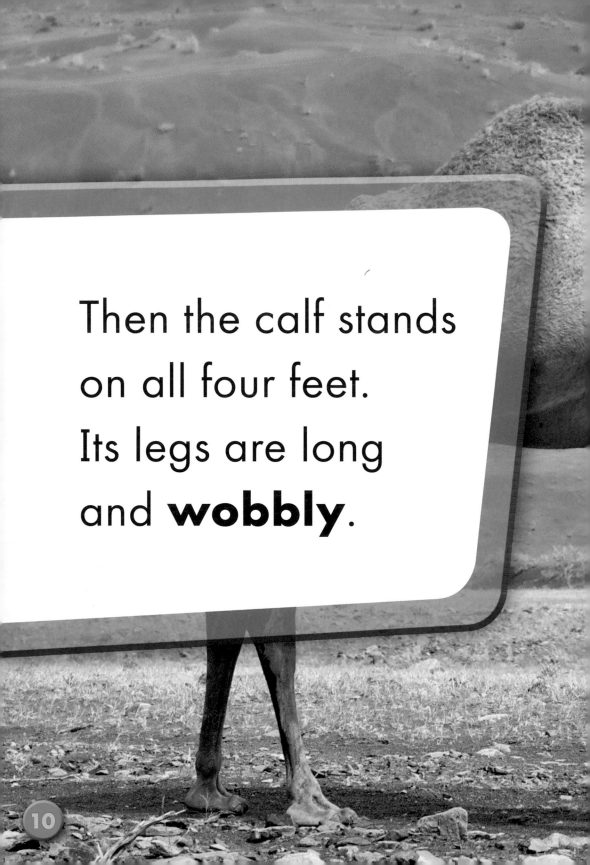

Then the calf stands
on all four feet.
Its legs are long
and **wobbly**.

Soon the calf can walk with mom. It is about 3 feet (1 meter) tall.

Mom and her calf join the **herd** after about two weeks.

14

Eating

The calf **bleats** to mom when hungry. It **nurses** for up to two years.

It also eats
grasses, leaves,
and twigs.

Now the calf's **humps** will start to grow!

21

Glossary

bleats—makes a noise that sounds like a shaky cry

herd—a group of camels that travel together

humps—the bumps on a camel's back; camels have one or two humps.

newborn—just recently born

nurses—drinks mom's milk

nuzzles—softly rubs up against with the nose or forehead

wobbly—shaky

wool—soft, thick hair

To Learn More

AT THE LIBRARY

Borgert-Spaniol, Megan. *Camels*.
Minneapolis, Minn.: Bellwether Media, 2012.

Riggs, Kate. *Camels*. Mankato, Minn.:
Creative Education, 2014.

Williams, Garth. *Baby Animals*. New York,
N.Y.: Golden Books, 2009.

ON THE WEB

Learning more about camels
is as easy as 1, 2, 3.

1. Go to www.factsurfer.com.

2. Enter "camels" into the search box.

3. Click the "Surf" button and you will see a
   list of related web sites.

With factsurfer.com, finding more information
is just a click away.

Index

The images in this book are reproduced through the courtesy of: Zzvet, front cover; Andrea Willmore, pp. 4-5; belizar, pp. 6-7, 8-9 (top); Vensk_Nadiya, pp. 8-9 (bottom); David Steele, pp. 10-11, 14-15, 16-17; Megapress/ Alamy, pp. 12-13; Arctic, pp. 18-19 (top); YolLusZam1802, pp. 18-19 (bottom); Krys Bailey/ Alamy, pp. 20-21.